ANTI-STRESS
COLORING BOOK
SACRED GEOMETRY

Easter Eggs

Copyright @2020 Eostre Ostara

All rights reserved. No part of this publication may be reproduced in any form or by any means without permission in writing by the author. No part can be reproduced, stored, or transmitted in any form or by any means, electronic, mechanical, photocopying, recording, scanning, or otherwise except as permitted with the permission of the author.

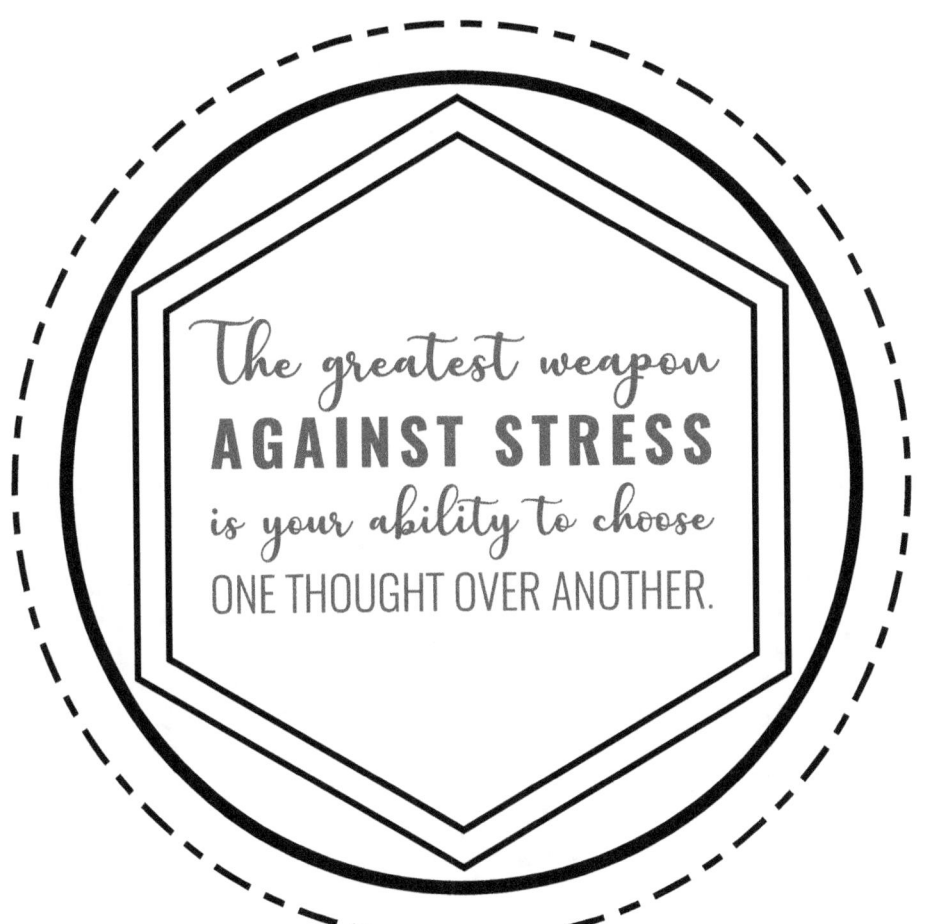

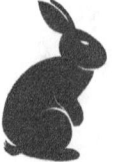

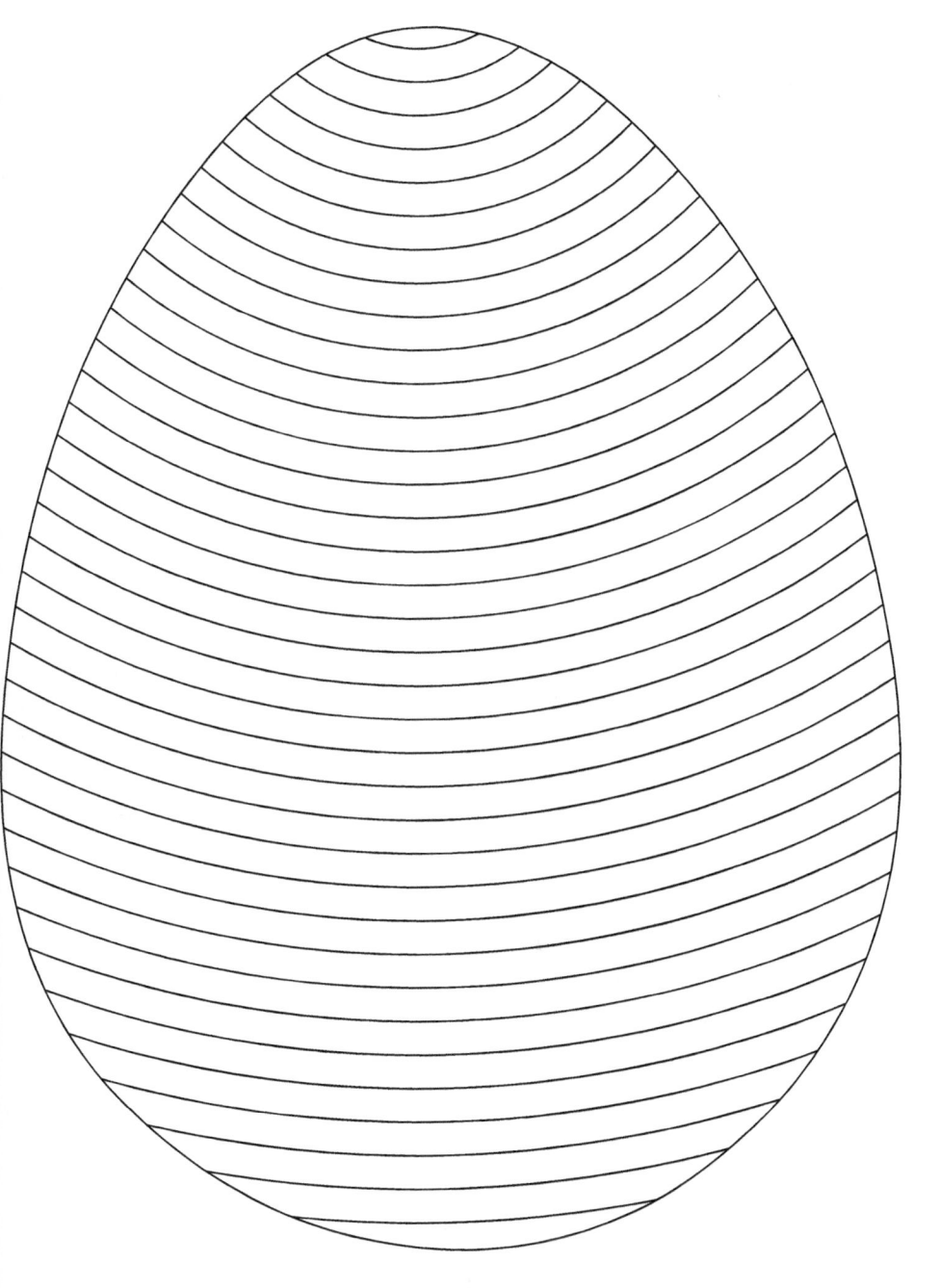

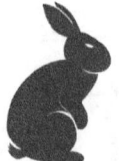

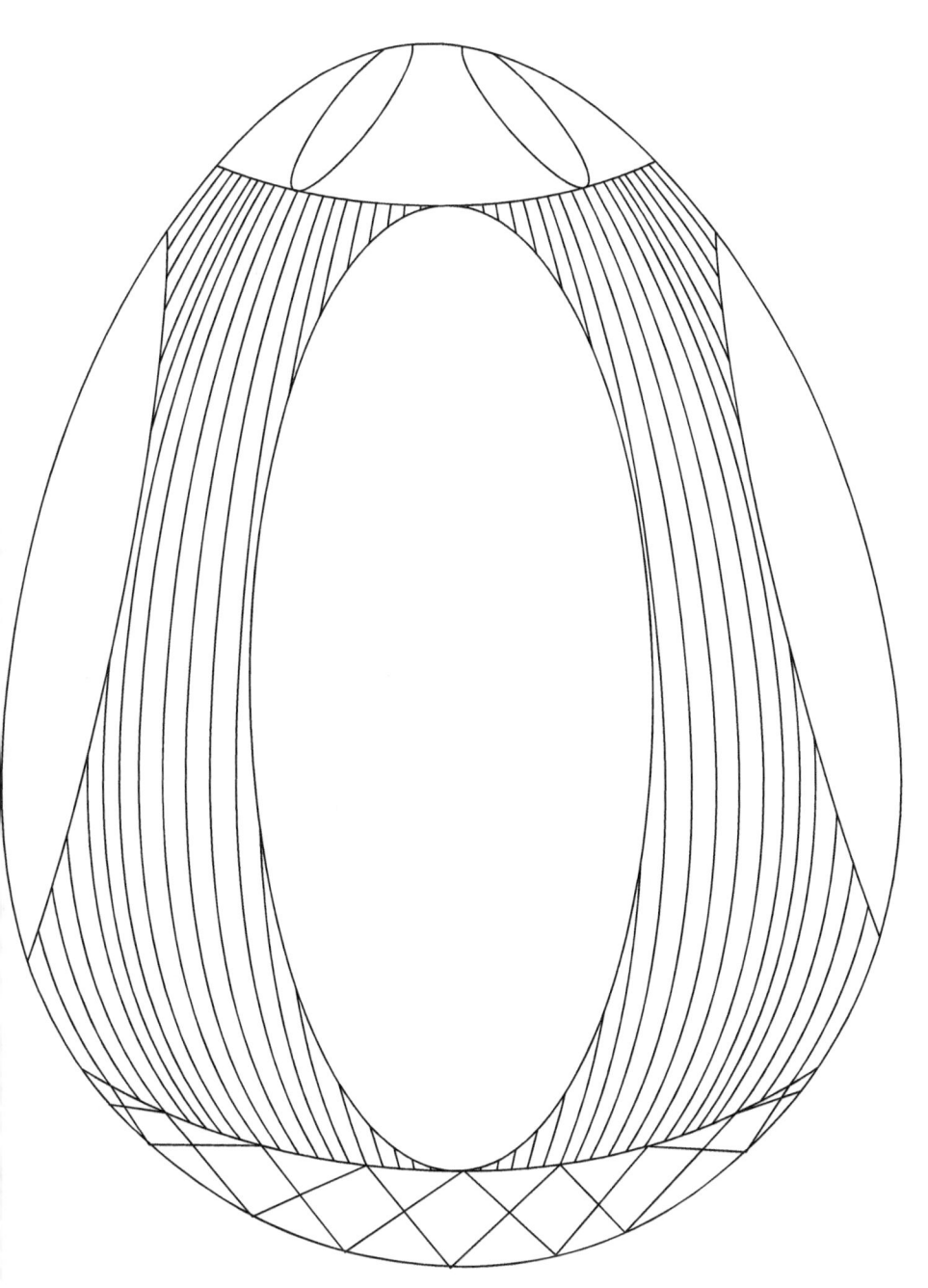

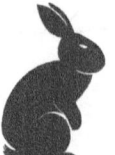

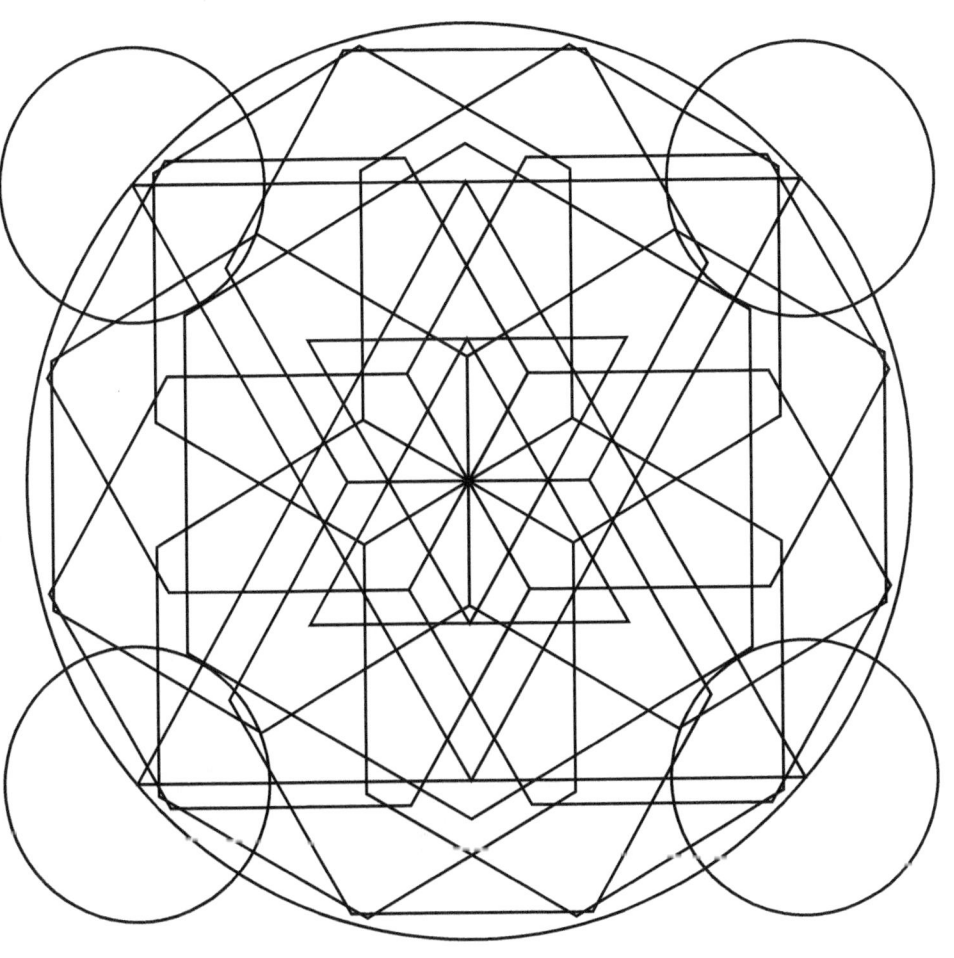

"YOU MUST LEARN TO LET GO. RELEASE THE STRESS. YOU WERE NEVER IN CONTROL ANYWAY."

- Steve Maraboli,
Life, the Truth, and Being Free

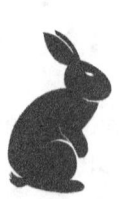

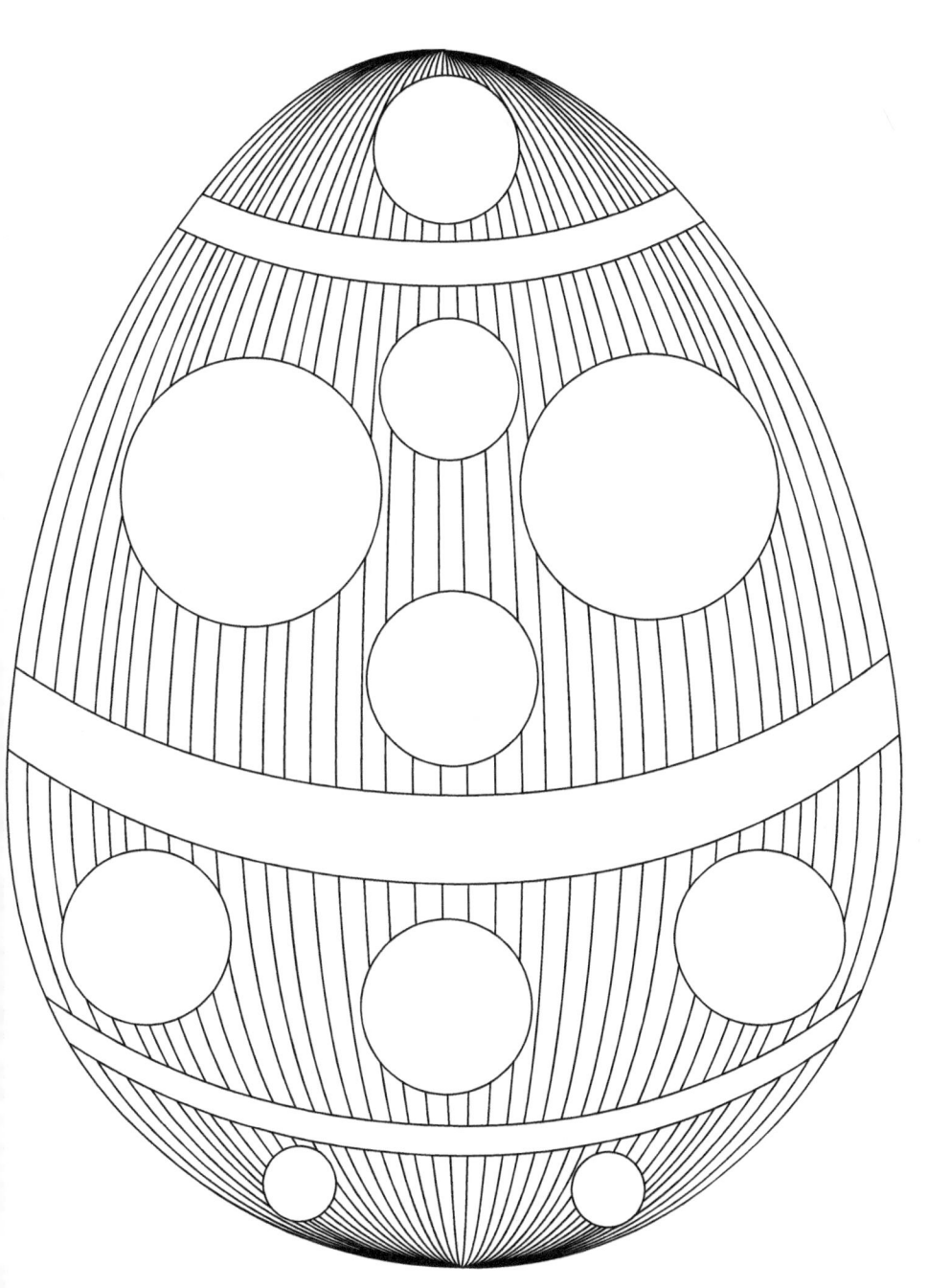

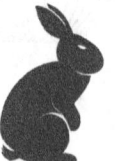

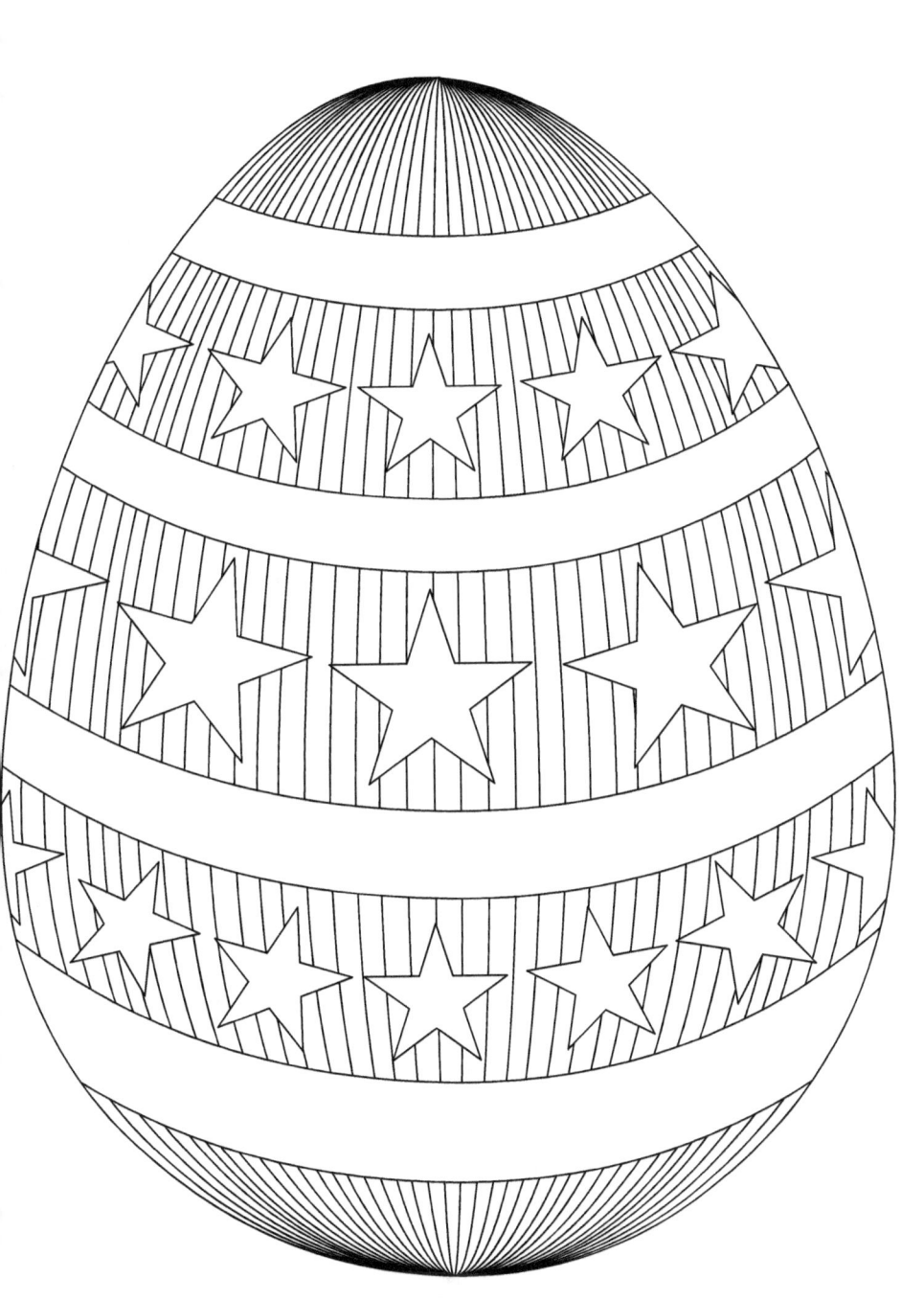

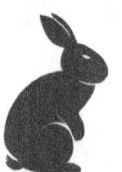

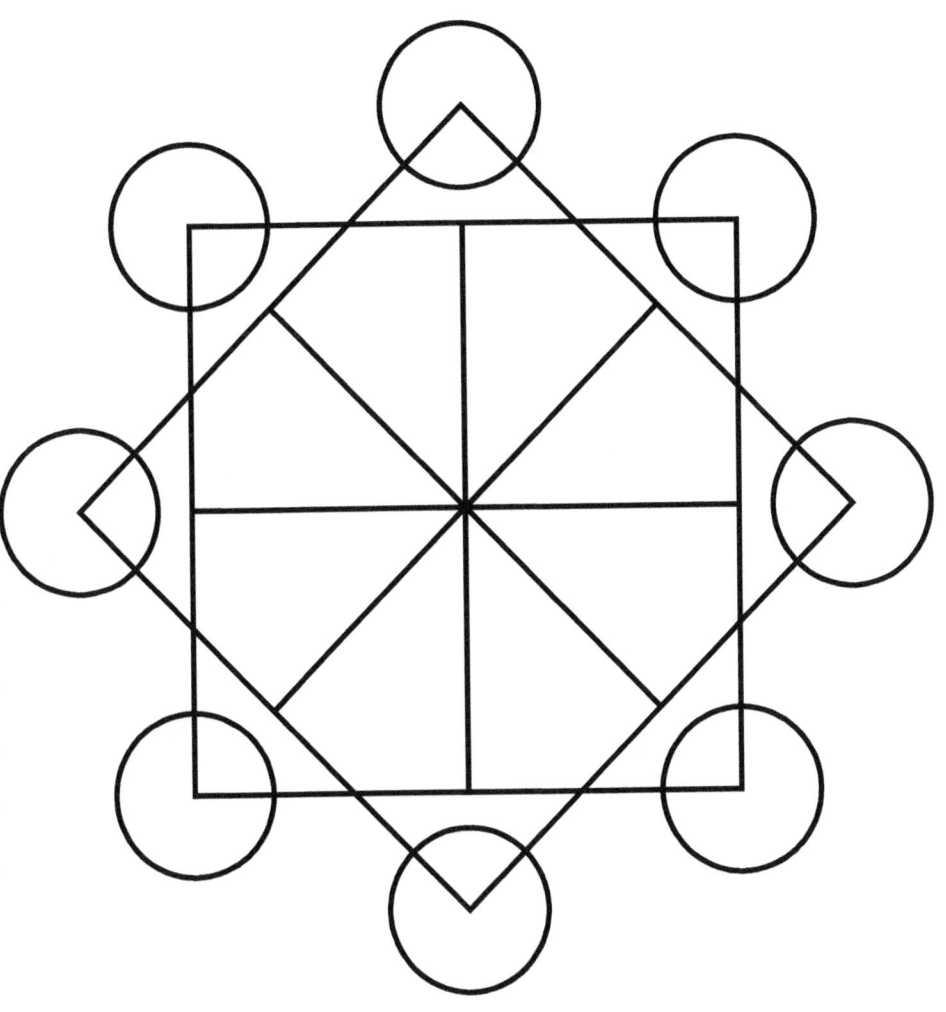

"IF YOU WANT TO CONQUER THE ANXIETY OF LIFE, LIVE IN THE MOMENT, LIVE IN THE BREATH."

- Amit Ray,
Om Chanting and Meditation

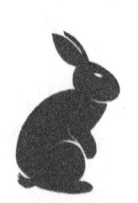

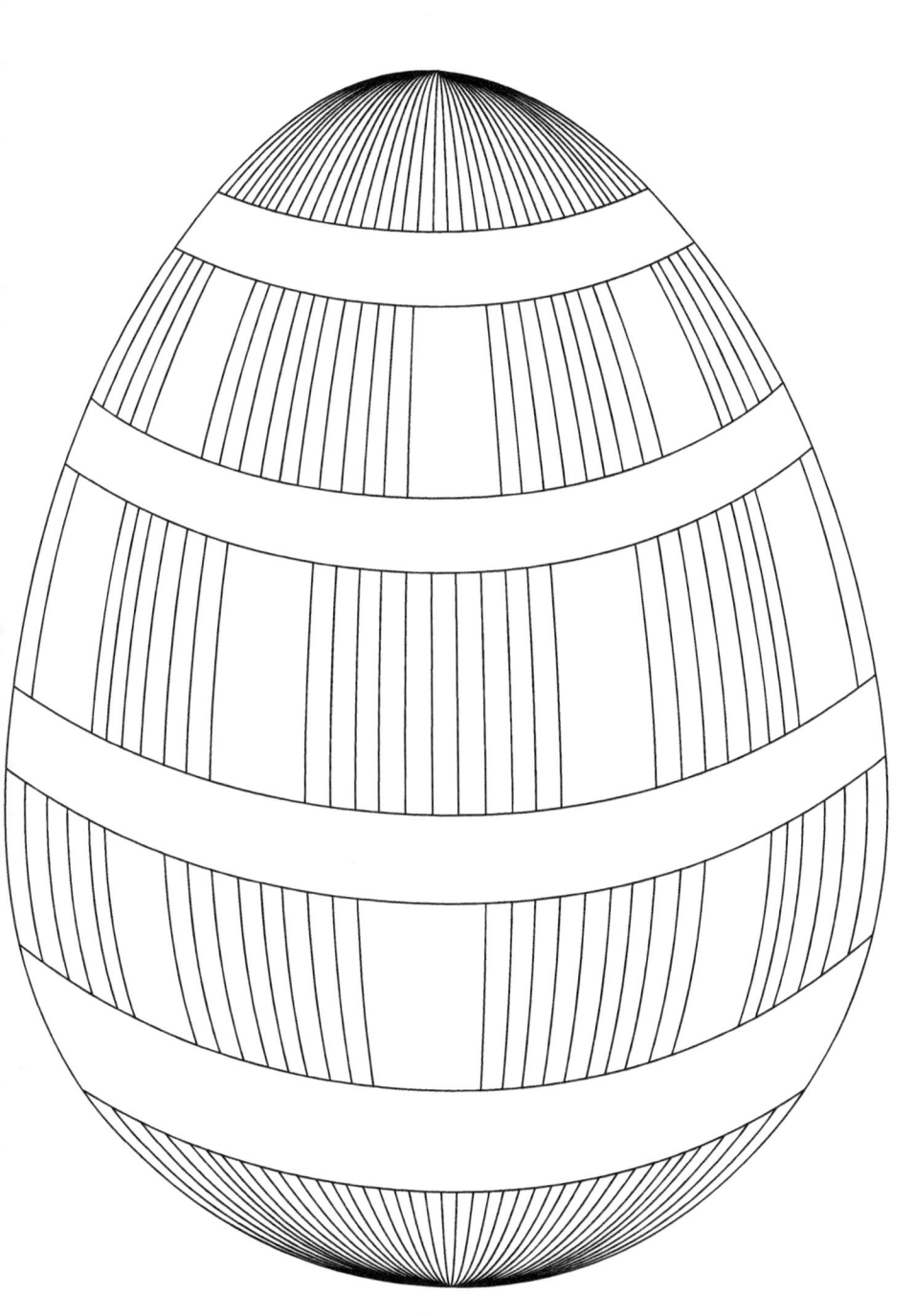

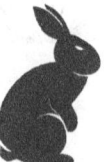

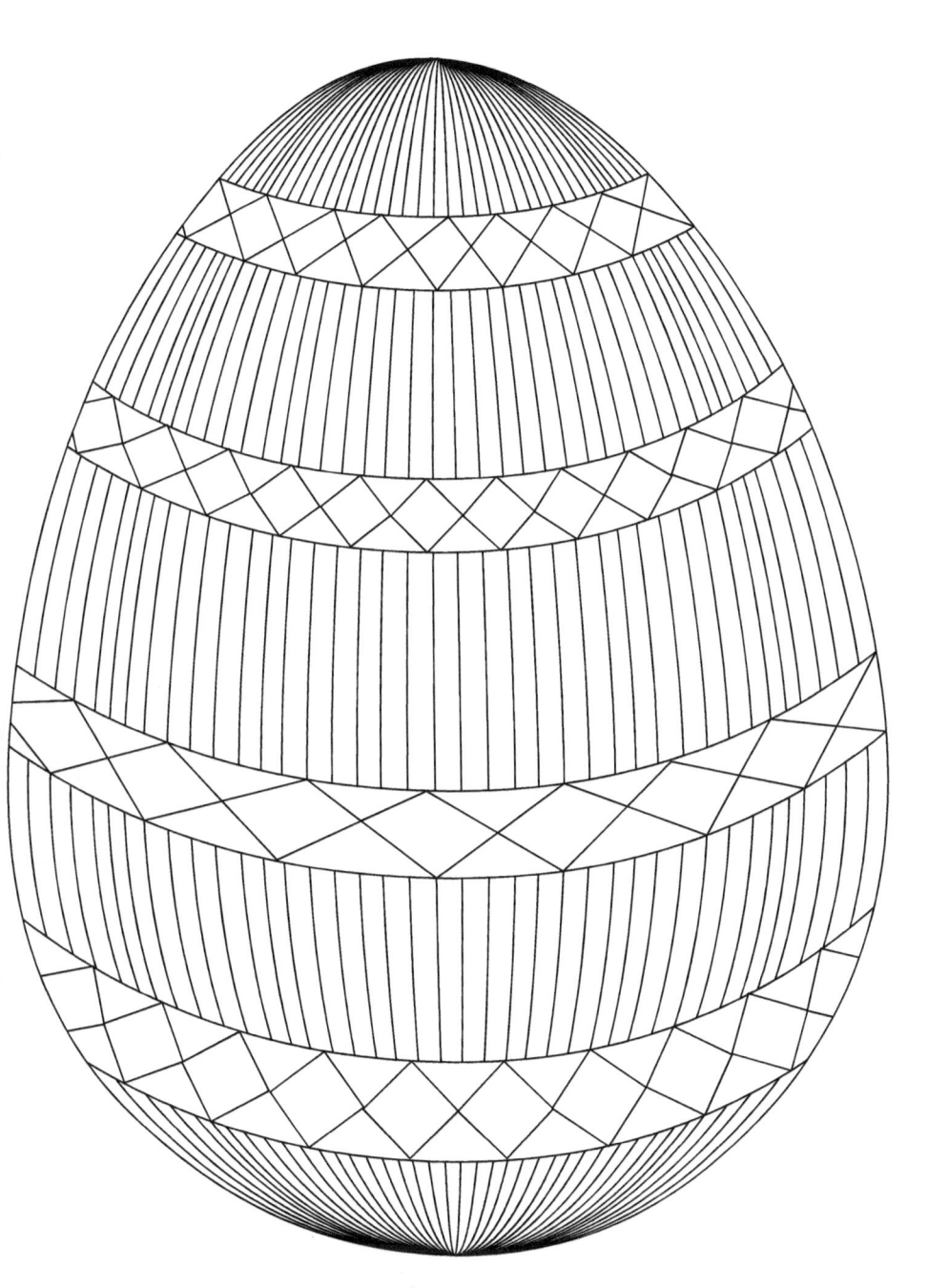

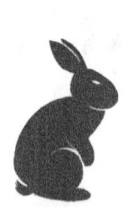

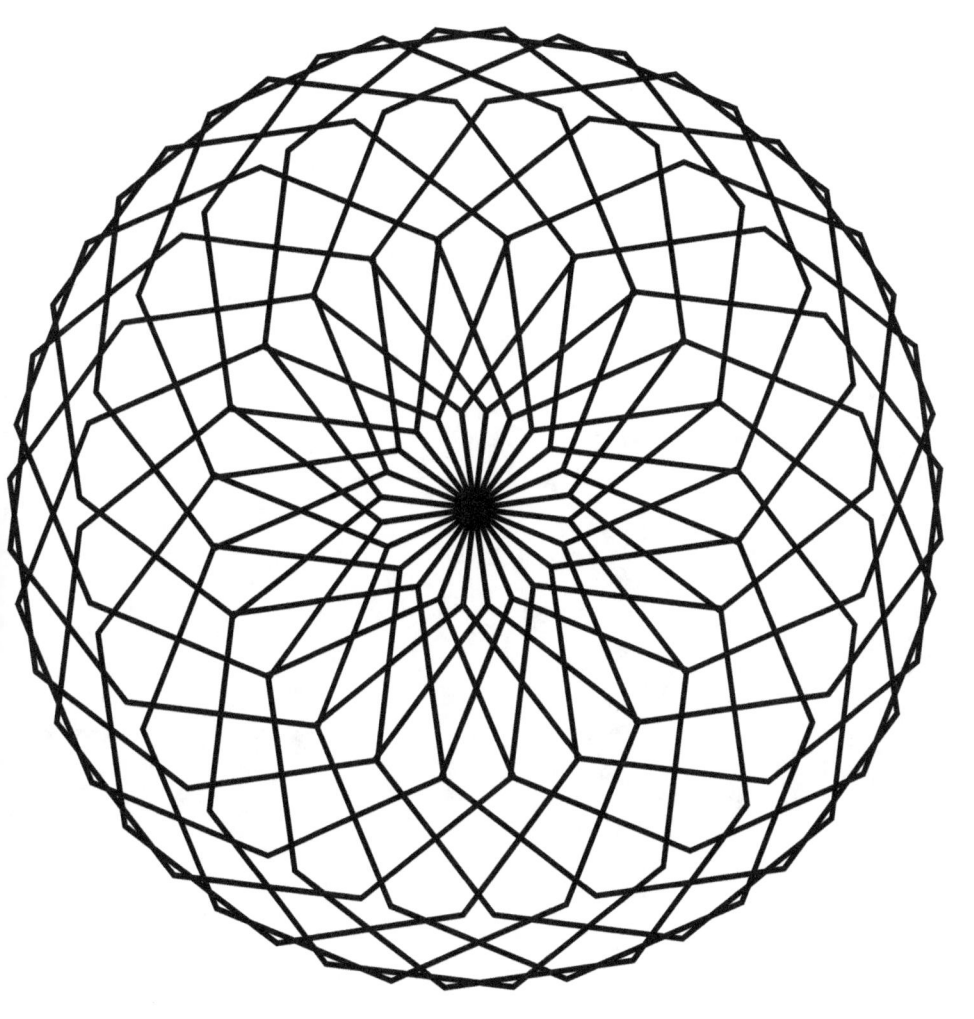

"WE MUST HAVE A PIE. STRESS CANNOT EXIST IN THE PRESENCE OF A PIE."

- David Mamet,
Boston Marriage

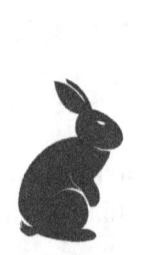

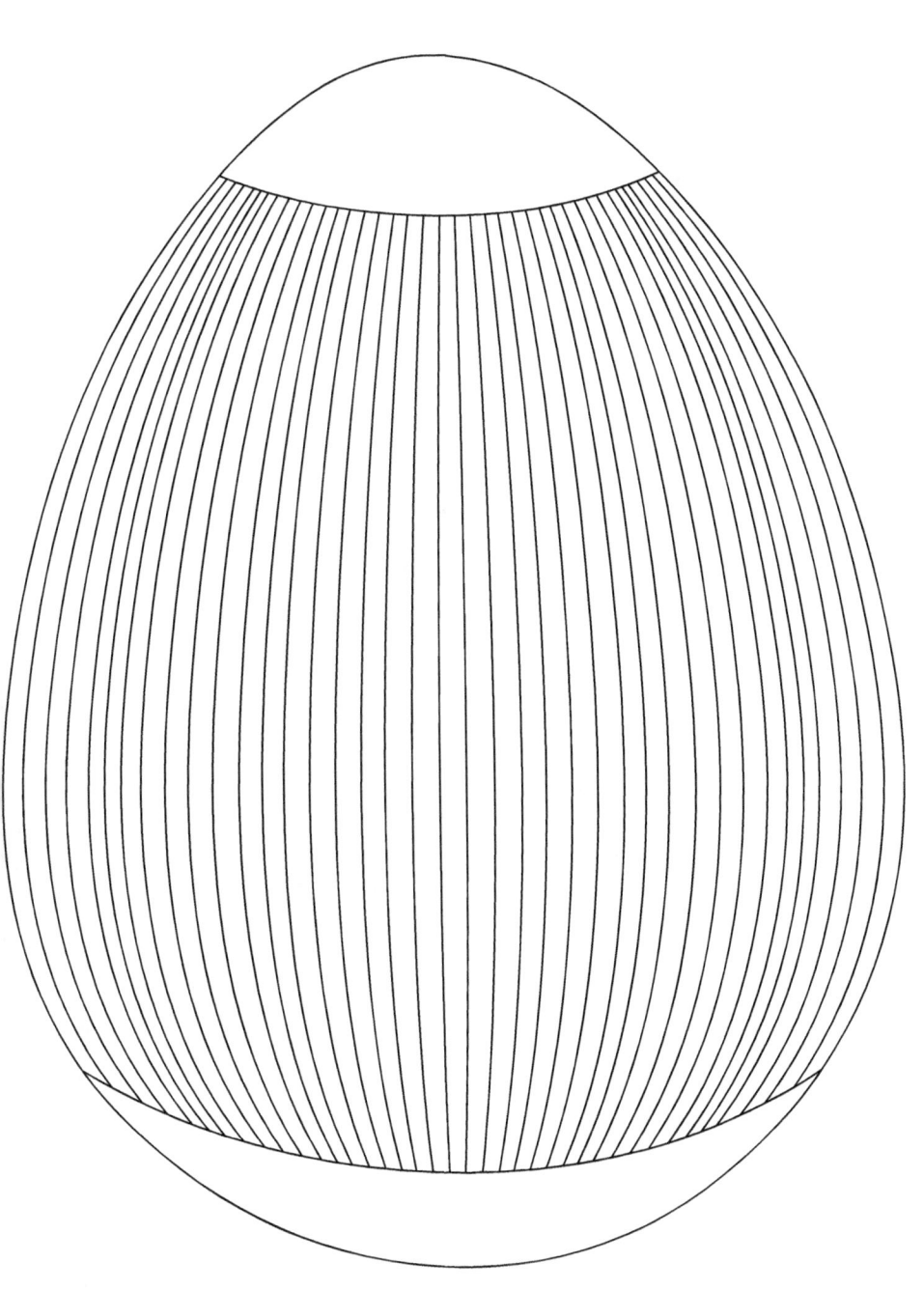

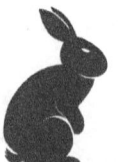

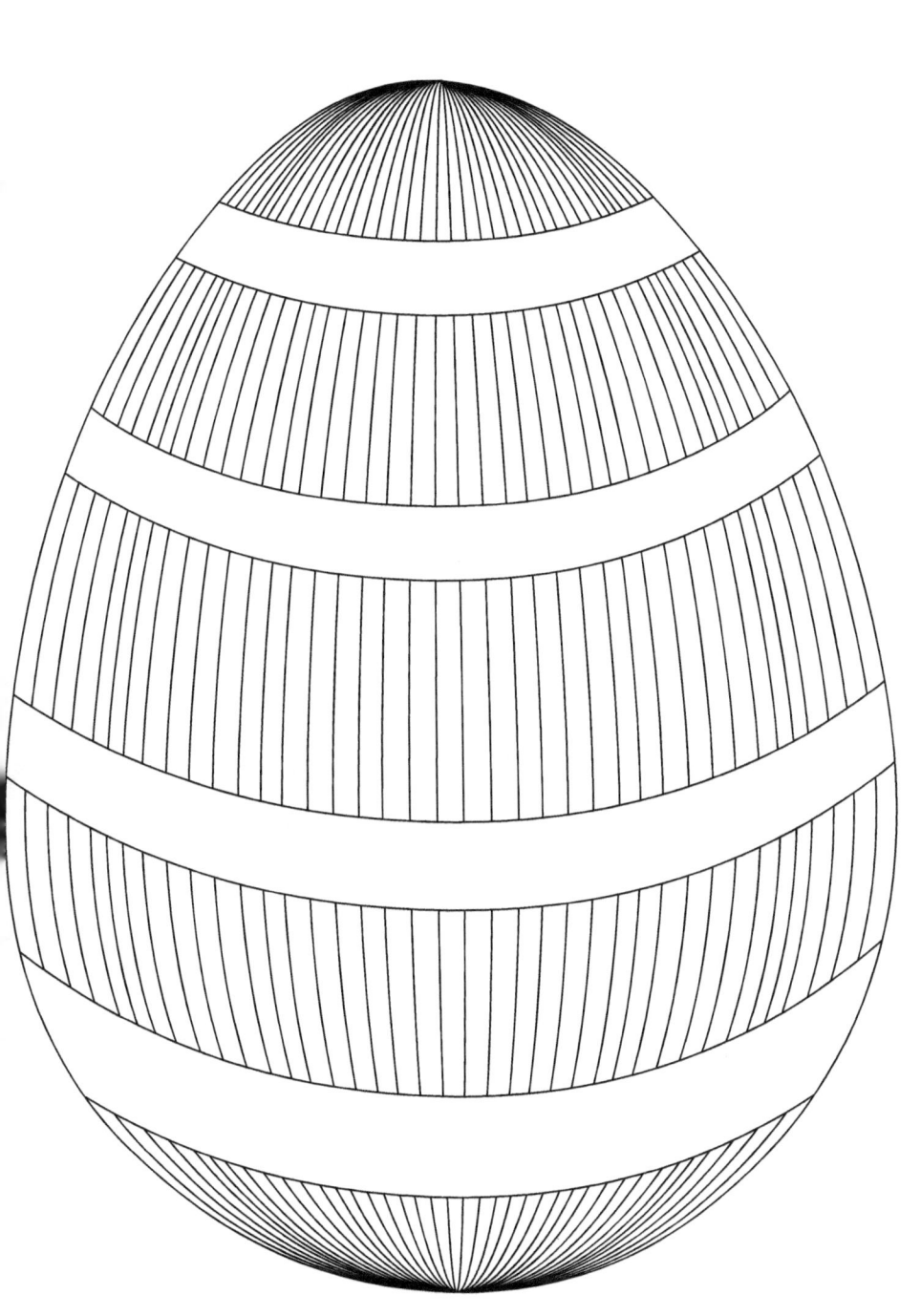

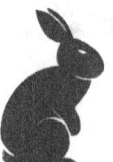

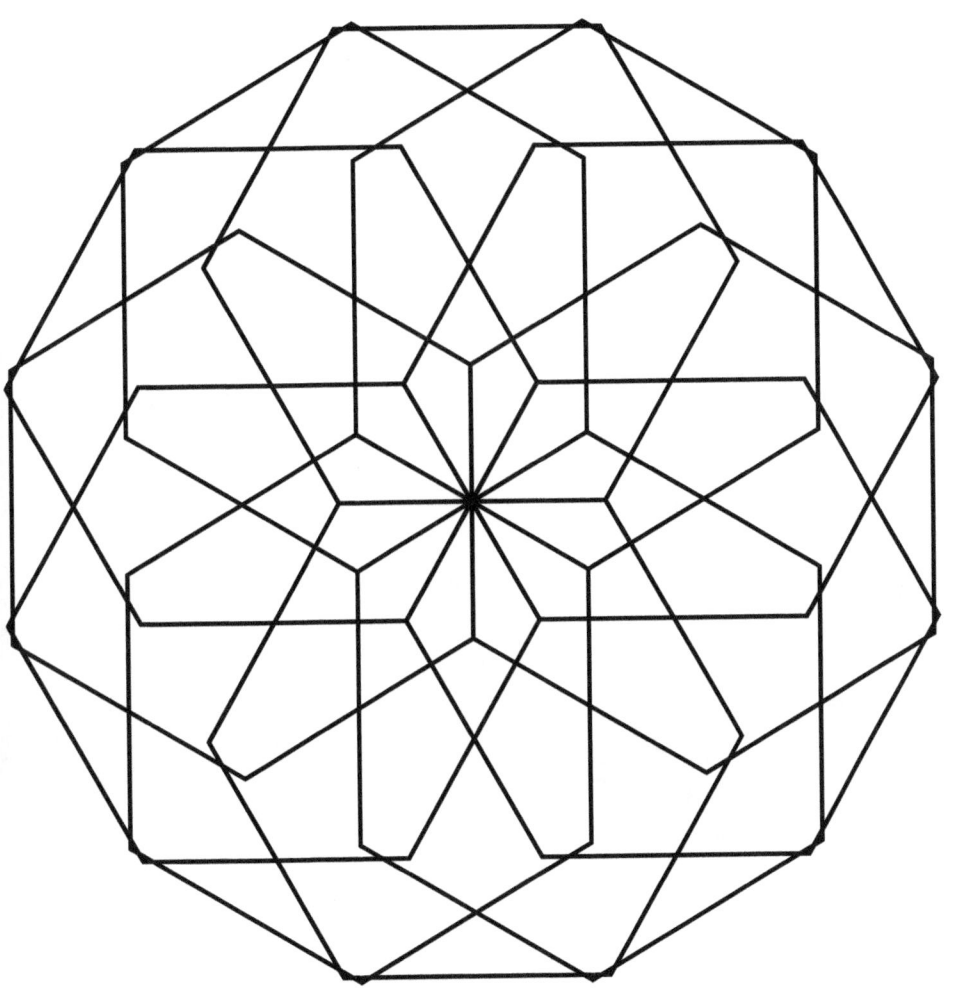

"TO ACHIEVE GREAT THINGS,
TWO THINGS ARE NEEDED:
A PLAN AND NOT QUITE ENOUGH TIME."

- Leonard Bernstein

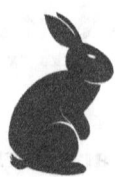

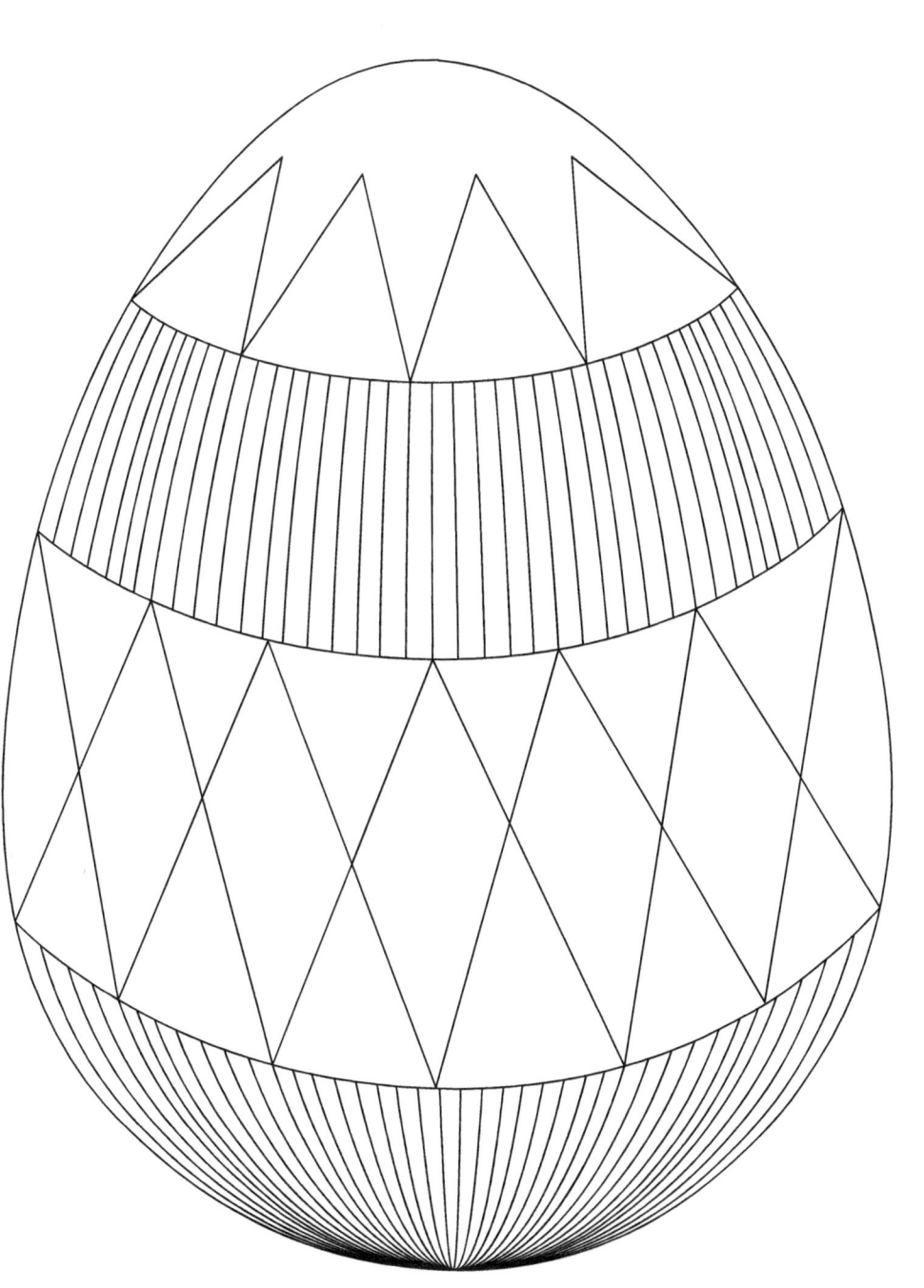

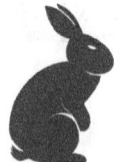

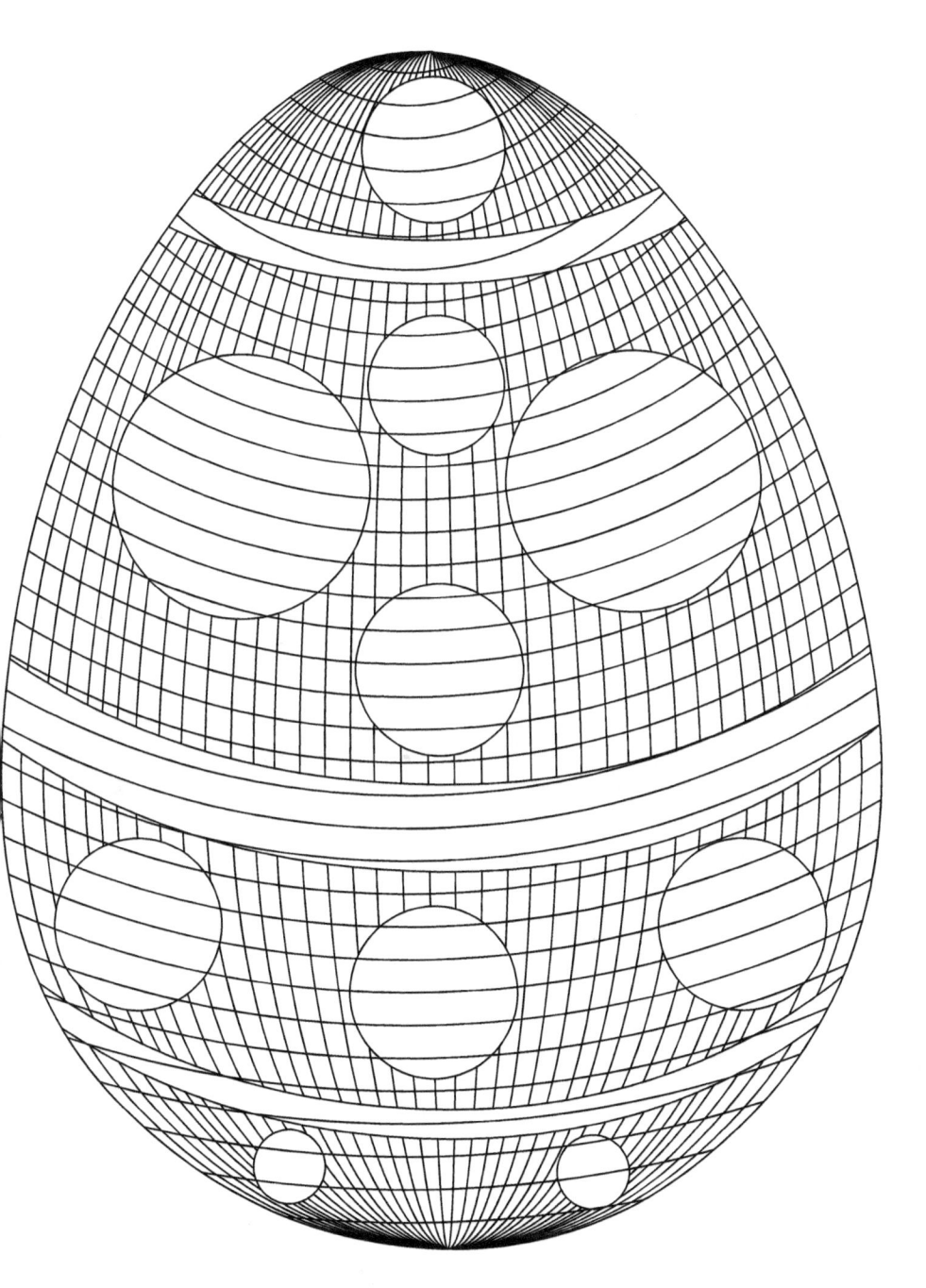

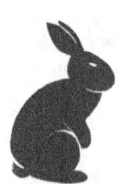

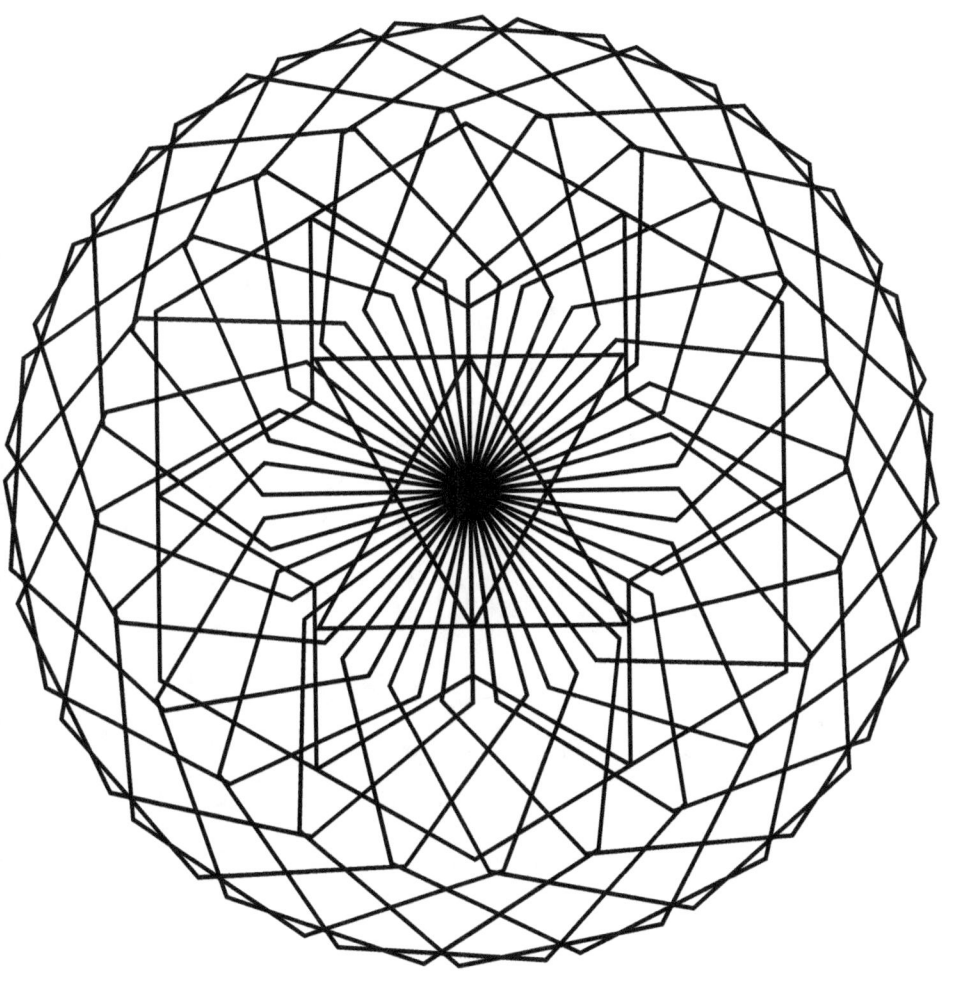

"IN TIMES OF STRESS, THE BEST THING WE CAN DO FOR EACH OTHER IS TO LISTEN WITH OUR EARS AND OUR HEARTS AND TO BE ASSURED THAT OUR QUESTIONS ARE JUST AS IMPORTANT AS OUR ANSWERS."

- Fred Rogers

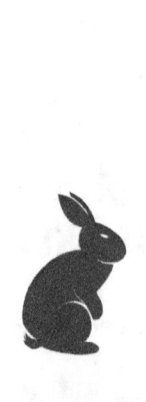

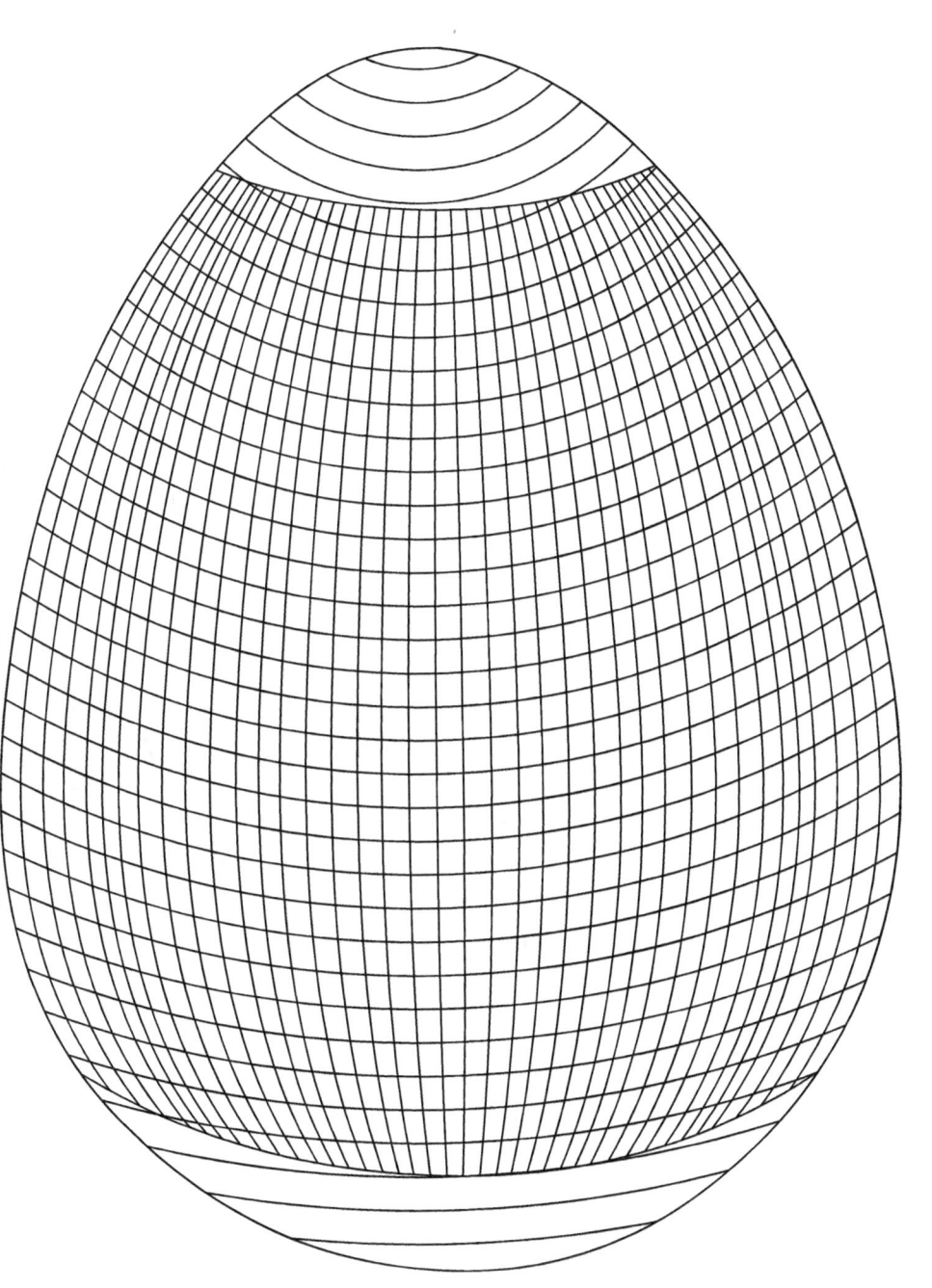

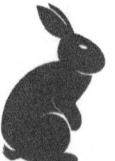

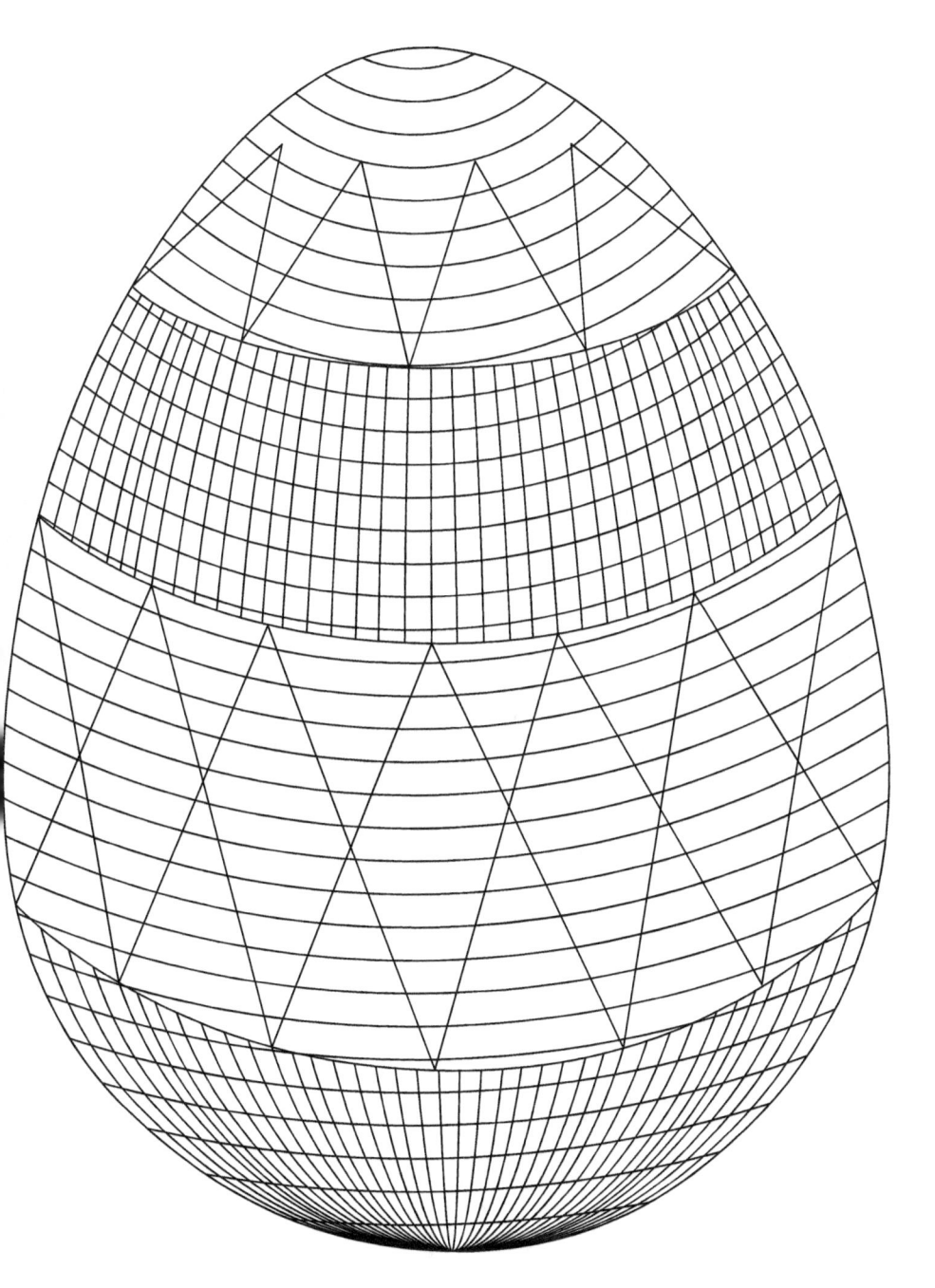

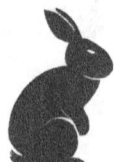

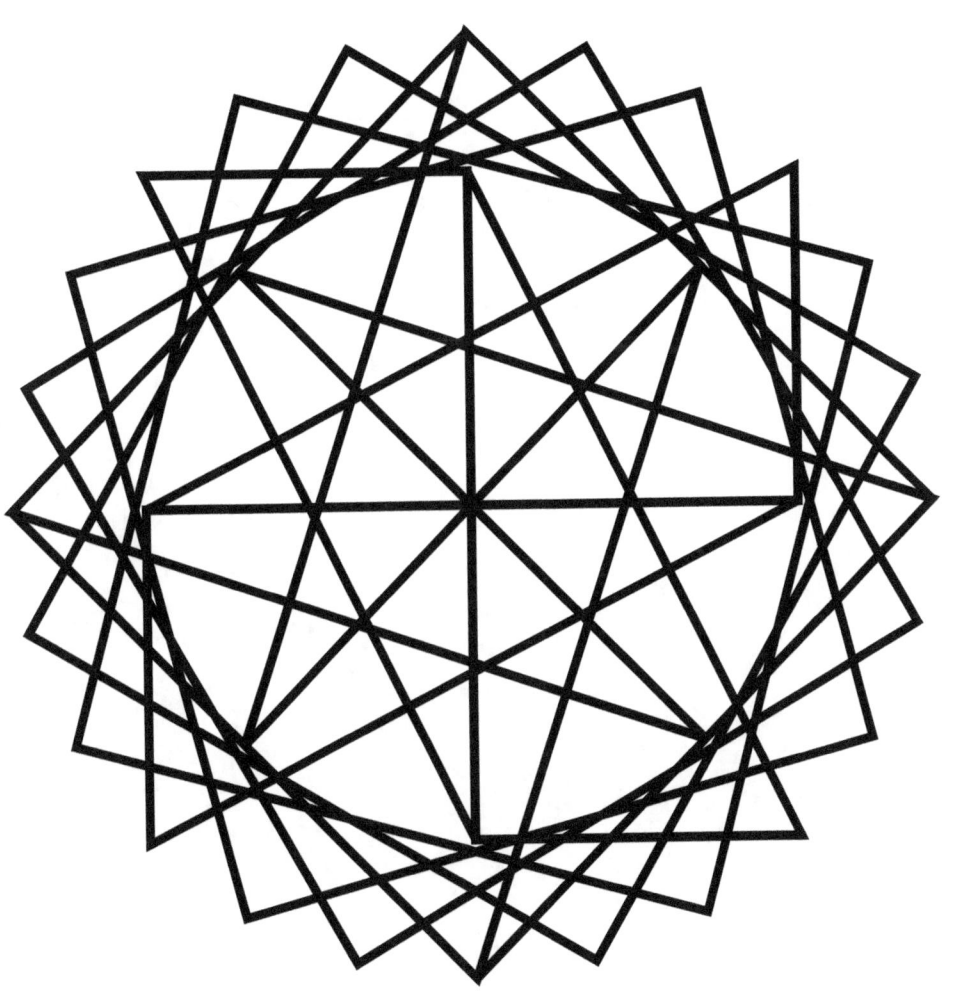

"I PROMISE YOU NOTHING IS AS CHAOTIC AS IT SEEMS. NOTHING IS WORTH DIMINISHING YOUR HEALTH. NOTHING IS WORTH POISONING YOURSELF INTO STRESS, ANXIETY, AND FEAR."

- Steve Maraboli

www.ingramcontent.com/pod-product-compliance
Lightning Source LLC
Chambersburg PA
CBHW070904220526
45466CB00005B/2124